D0539850

THE WASTING GAME

TONBRIDGE SCHOOL LIBRARY

R16963M0502

Philip Gross was born in 1952 in Delabole, Cornwall, and grew up in Plymouth. Since moving to Bristol in 1984, he has been a freelance writer and writing tutor, performing and visiting schools, and teaches on the Creative Studies programme at Bath Spa University College.

He won a Gregory Award in 1981 and first prize in the National Poetry Competition in 1982. Since then he has published poetry for adults – *Familiars* (Peterloo, 1983), *The Ice Factory* (Faber, 1984), *Cat's Whisker* (Faber, 1987), *The Air Mines of Mistila* (with Sylvia Kantaris, Bloodaxe Books, 1988: Poetry Book Society Choice), *The Son of the Duke of Nowhere* (Faber, 1991), *I.D.* (Faber, 1994) and *The Wasting Game* (Bloodaxe Books, 1998: Poetry Book Society Recommendation) – and for young people – *Manifold Manor* (Faber, 1989), *The All Nite Café* (Faber, 1993: winner of the Signal Award 1994) and *Scratch City* (Faber, 1995). His collaborations with artists include *A Cast of Stones* (Digging Deeper, June 1996) with John Eaves and F.J. Kennedy, *Nature Studies* (Yellow Fox Press, 1995) with Ros Cuthbert, and *Coniunctio: a spell* (Prospero Poets, 1995) with Vance Gerry. His children's opera *Snail Dreaming*, with music by composer Glyn Evans, was performed by the Britten Sinfonietta in 1997.

His first novel for young people was *The Song of Gail and Fludd* (Faber, 1991). Since then Scholastic have published four more novels for teenagers, *Plex* (1994), *The Wind Gate* (1995), *Transformer* (1996) and *Psylicon Beach* (1998). His radio play *Internal Affairs* won the BBC West of England Playwriting Competition in 1986 – and a stage play, *Rising Star*, had its first airing from Show of Strength in 1996. An adult novel is in progress.

PHILIP GROSS

the wasting game

BLOODAXE BOOKS

Copyright © Philip Gross 1998

ISBN: 1 85224 479 8

First published 1998 by
Bloodaxe Books Ltd,
P.O. Box 1SN,
Newcastle upon Tyne NE99 1SN.

Bloodaxe Books Ltd acknowledges
the financial assistance of Northern Arts.

LEGAL NOTICE

All rights reserved. No part of this book may be
reproduced, stored in a retrieval system, or
transmitted in any form, or by any means, electronic,
mechanical, photocopying, recording or otherwise,
without prior written permission from Bloodaxe Books Ltd.

Requests to publish work from this book
must be sent to Bloodaxe Books Ltd.

Philip Gross has asserted his right under
Section 77 of the Copyright, Designs and Patents Act 1988
to be identified as the author of this work.

R16963
821.914

Cover printing by J. Thomson Colour Printers Ltd, Glasgow.

Printed in Great Britain by
Cromwell Press Ltd, Trowbridge, Wiltshire.

Acknowledgements

Acknowledgments are due to the editors of the following publications in which some of these poems first appeared: *Envoi, The Independent, Links, London Magazine, Looming* (Tallinn), *Modern Painters, Nature Studies* (Yellow Fox Press, with illustrations by Ros Cuthbert), *The North, Obsessed With Pipework, A Parcel of Poems* (Faber, for Ted Hughes), *Poetry London Newsletter, Poetry Review, Poetry Wales, The Poet's Voice, Resurgence, The Rialto, Spectator, Stand, Times Educational Supplement, Thumbscrew* and *The Times Literary Supplement.*

'Gargangel' won first prize in the Peterloo Poets Open Competition in 1998. Acknowledgements are due also to the judges of the Exeter Poetry Competition (for 'Visiting Persephone'), the Blue Nose Poet of the Year Award (for 'The Wasting Game') and the Peterloo Poets Open Competition (for 'Trebizond').

Thanks are due to Bath Spa University College, the British Council, UNESCO and Doris Kareva for making my visits to Estonia possible.

And to Rosemary, love and respect.

Contents

Visiting Persephone

Can you picture *him*
going down to see her, fitting in
with the difficult visiting times?
He was her father, after all.

But to enter that dark,
that mould and mouldering, his power
and glory threatening to wink out
like a fused bulb with a pinging whine

would tax a better god than him.
She is yellowish pale this week
with a drained look, no pink
but some fresh scars on her arm,

the others aged to shrivelled plum.
She has keelhauled herself by inches
or been crawling down narrowing
ducts of slime and shale.

Some days she hardly greets him
and her silence is a waiting room
where he sits and is not called for,
feeling younger than she is, learning

to make out the shapes in her gloom.
The gifts he foisted on her
leave him dull, a Souza march
come shuffling to a halt

outside the darkened concert hall
where a child's violin
slips on difficult scales,
then you look and there's no one.

He gets up to go, go
where? How could he have imagined
he was any sort of god? How could he
have imagined this at all?

The Wasting Game

1

'I'm fat, look, *fat*...'

Yes and the moon's made of cheese,
that chunk she won't touch in the fridge

dried, creviced, sweating in its cold
like someone with a killing fever.

Half a scrape-of-marmite sandwich,
last night's pushed-aside

potatoes greying like a tramp's teeth,
crusts, crumbs are a danger to her,

so much orbiting space junk
that's weightless for only so long.

Burn it up on re-entry, burn it,
burn it. So she trains

with weights, she jogs, she runs
as if the sky were falling.

2

Curled like a lip, a crust dries in the bin,
the supermodel's come-on-don't-touch sneer
for the camera – desire
caught, teased, time and again

till all the wants run dry
and there's only this rictus,
a cat raking claws
down the arm of the chair,

eyes closed, lips apart
like the girl's head she drew
arching back to a lover's long
bone fingers tangled in her hair.

3

The eating thing:

the slouching beast
that's come to stay,

to spatter the slops
and foul the manger,

to snap at the hand
that tries to feed it, so

we leave it and we lie
in darkness, trying not to know,

not to hear it gnawing
in the next room, gnawing

itself to the bone.

4

Dry priestess at the shrine
of nothing. Maid-saint
fierce against the flesh
(burn it, burn it) denouncing
the witch in herself, see,
she's mounting the stake,
no, *becoming* it *and*
the tinder and the heartless
blaze you might mistake
for holiness. My homegrown
Manichee, almost 'perfected'

as the Cathars had it
fasting unto death. 'I want
a perfect figure.' Saying no
to the pull of the world.
Straight out, she said it
(burning but not yet
consumed) she said 'Weight
is bad. Bad.' On the blanket.
In the desert of her bed.

5

To be perfect...? 'Nothing's
perfect in this life,' I say.

Mealy middle-aged wisdom,

eat your words. See how
precisely she'll come to agree.

6

Close now, this nothing-

hungry thing that fills
her, that empties her... Once

in aquarium twilight a grey-
silver bass brought a face

big as mine up to the glass,
chewing water, with the weight

of deep ocean behind it. The cold.
Its tuppenny eye had a gleam

like contempt. For me? Or worse:
maybe its own reflection in the glass

was all it saw?

7

It's the Dark Ages now. I believe
in possession, in demons that speak
in crone voices out of fifteen-year-old lips,

her lips that have taken a tuck in
at the corner, a small crease like age
or disapproval when she (seldom) smiles.

I believe fairy tales like hot news,
how the Snow Queen's pinched
enraptured child might desire

nothing but to spell ETERNITY
from jags of ice, how Rumpelstiltskin
with the rage of any secret thing

that's named for what it is
might stamp so hard the splintering
could go on for ever,

how the scientists at Los Alamos
watched the fireball grow
and thought: it might not stop,

it might consume us all.

8

She's been paying her dues to gravity
in dud coin once a week

checking in on the doctor's scales
which wobble to a judgment: *holding steady*

though she's less and less able to hoist
what mass she still has, and she sways,

the rush of faintness in her ears like sea
hissing in over mud and in and in

as she steadies herself and walks towards it
with stones in her pockets, adding one a week.

9

Inside her, the slowing,
the faltering
voltage.
But still

there's this brilliant
flicker on the surface,
arc lights
on a dragged canal,

moving pictures
that don't quite
finesse the eye;
there are moments

you almost see through
(freeze *there*)
when the screen
shows nothing but a grey

room and gradually
shapes, near-transparent,
near-familiar,
like the threadbare home video

mailed with impossible demands.
You see the hostages,
a family,
staring out at you.

10

Ketones: a sour chemical smell on her skin
like a darkroom with blackouts on windows,
with shallow trays of fluid silky-still
as a swimming pool after lights-out,
their monochromes hardening. Developed,
they will close the family album.

11

I could hate

those frail maids fading beautifully
in books, wax lilies, pale-succulent

stalks that might snap
at a touch. The bird-dropping of blood

in a lace-bordered handkerchief
like the monstrance on the nuptual sheet.

A consummation most devoutly wished
by death. The maiden turns,

in woodcuts from another age
of plagues, to his knuckleboned touch,

half smiling; the consumptive turns
on her lace-bordered pillow

weakly and away
from any warmth of flesh

as if stung; the anorexic turns
her face towards these stories, stories

which, because I love the girl,
I hate.

12

She left home months ago.
Somehow we never noticed.
She was going solo

as a conjuror:
the egg we found rotting
in the body-folds of the sofa;

caked wads
of tissues in the bin with weetabix
compacted in them like the Mob's

car-crusher sandwiches;
potatoes spirited away
with one pass of the baggy-wristed

sweater she draped
on her bones. (What applause
when she whips it off one day

and she's gone!) Co-ordination
slipping now, caught out –
fraud, fraud! –

she plays the cheapest trick of all.
A toothmug of tap water,
sixty paracetamol.

She tries hissing herself offstage.

13

Drip. Drip.

Those stripped
twigs of her fingers.
Ivy torsions in the wrist.

Two spikes bandaged
to drip in her veins.

Sap sunk
at fifteen, she's been old
for too long, always cold
in her matt blacks, always
in some sort of mourning.

Mulched like leafmould,
mushroom-breathed, shit-smelling,
she's a question: Can
you love this?
Can you sit

and watch the hours dissolving
in the drip
of Parvolax and glucose
clear as rinsings from bare twig tips
when the downpour's gone?

They're trying to wash the river
in her blood. They're on the phone
to the Poisons Unit:
the readings aren't clear.
Nothing's perfect

but it's all there is.
This. Now. The drip
of plain words. Yes.
Love.
This.

Imago

She spent winter and spring
in her chrysalis, a strait world
shrunk and puckered like a mis-stitched scar.

Inside it held a breaking down of things
like a drop of original swamp sea.
Which is one way not to speak

of unopening windows resigned to the view
of the CAUTION PATIENTS CROSSING
speedbumped drive; the coded sign

NO CASUALTY DEPARTMENT here
among so many casualties;
the swabbed smells and the sounds off

like that sobbing on legs
down the corridor, and the dribbling
overspill from the padlocked pool

where a green beach ball scuds slow
eccentric orbits
to the pipe and back and round...

                    *

Hawk moth caterpillars
dropped from the limes in our street,
pointless manna she'd save

like the good girl she was,
on damp earth in a jam-jar.
They shrank to sealed flasks

for the usual great experiment.
We found a blood-brown drip
in the husk where one vanished;

another that, shrink-
wrapped too tight in itself,
couldn't ever split free.

So seeing her now
rise from the station subway
with bags marked for home,

to the lip of the crowd, and hesitate,
not a child now, and not any image
I could make to hold her,

I can't call her name,
I can't find words for her,
I wouldn't dare.

Trebizond

Some days nothing about him seems worth preserving.
He's a marker that slips from a library book

and who'll ever know who had to meet *Jenny*
at 3! or where or why the exclamation

or what pages their meeting was parting?
He's all footnotes, a boneyard of keys

at the back of the drawer as if their true
suitcases might come back to claim them.

He's all those rainy lunchtimes interleaved
between Classics and History when he'd been fourteen

for ever, working through to the last
appendix of *The Roman Empire in the East*,

to the last ragged flutter of purple
nailed to a last-ditch trading post in Asia Minor.

Some days nothing about him seems to justify
these leaps of faith: that Jenny met the one

with the key to her life; that you, dear Reader, you
might read this; that there's a hectare of stones

and goat-scrub where an old man wears a name
like *Kasar* or *Cezur* by direct succession

and his hayloft's a leafmould of edicts
rummaged from Byzantium; that the swot in the specs

might have made it past 1453. Some days
he just clings to a word, any word, say, *Trebizond*.

Tail

That's them: a soured-cream Escort
in the Tesco carpark. That's them
loading the bottle bank straight from the boot:

him and her, faces blanker
than stocking-masked bandits
as they play its holes like fruit machines,

without speaking or turning.
That's how many plonk bottles,
how many asking-a-few-friends-rounds

go down the hatch
with a blink of the flap. Smack of glass.
An after-quiver like a slammed piano.

Now the Escort nudges
into rank with fifty others,
noses in, rumps out like cows put to stud.

And now I'm waiting as the twitchy
reflex of the automatic doors
clocks them in. Let's quiz the loading bay

for clues: that leaning pagoda
of cardboard crates, the roulette sound
of a stout bottle rolling to and fro.

All circumstantial. But I'm close,
got what's left of the day
backed up against the wall

and each muffled shatter
from the bottle bank is me
ramming its head back: OK buddy,

spill the beans, thud,
are they *happy*? thud, thud, tell me
everything you know.

Thou'

A case of key and keyhole,
    us: what clicks

or doesn't in a place not seen
    until we're bits

dismantled, springs spilled everywhere;
    when edges crisp

as cornflakes once don't always kiss;
    what jams or slips

fumbled after the party, wrong door,
    sorry; what fits

in the gullet or sticks like a glove,
    depending how

precisely the spaces between us
are tooled –
            to a tolerance, let's say,
    of the nearest *thou'*.

thou': a thousandth of an inch (engineering).

Nineteenseventysomething

We Scotchtaped Cuban posters
round the attic walls. The wretched of the earth
made fists above us as we slept.
On damp nights they peeled slowly off
with a throat-clearing sound

like a more tactful hint than we deserved.
It was a house of all angles but right.
All the junk shops in Brighton
couldn't find furniture odd enough to fit.
Our chairs looked ill at ease, as if about to go.

When we pinned up our Indian bedspread,
pre-faded like jeans, it could have been
the clothes-horse tent I played house in
before they invented the Sixties.
Us, we'd never marry. We were outlaws

lying low, unscrewing the legs of our bed
against mother's advice. Turning back
from the smell of your body and mine
newly moistened like parched earth
I snuffed carpet dust and damp.

Nights made up most of that year .
And that voice through the wall from next door
where the curtains stayed shut.
Unseen, endless and scourging:
'Little bugger. I'll learn you...'

She was our age or less,
her four-year-old inaudible,
nearly invisible even when we saw him
and we had no words for this either
so came round to not mentioning it

but got into heavier music, Led Zep,
Wishbone Ash, and got on with the loss
of our childhoods, at leisure, urgently
before our grants ran out.
It never crossed our minds that we'd begun.

Spirit Level

Here on the sinking edge of England
the stones range from hipjoints to knucklebones.
There's a scarp drop, then the North Sea
    cants uphill and how
the tankers tightropewalk that skyline
is beyond me; I'm wobbly as the bubble
in a spirit level, ungrounded, and nothing's
    quite straight or quite true.
The Ness is a name and a notion, shifty
as the North Magnetic Pole. I've walked since teatime,
dogged as a number-crunching mainframe
    on its quest for God
rounded down to the Highest Prime Number;
the coast slips away round the corner for ever
in front and behind. It could shrug us all off
    into space: me,
this toy village with its late-night postcard shop,
this house like the fo'c'sle of a beached brigantine
with uncaulked planks that would rot in a year
    (or so the landlord says)
if it weren't for the draughts; that single car
on the front where a glow like cave moss up
from the dashboard lights two faces, lovers
    who have come to sit
and not speak and stare opposite ways.
Both ways, the sea is coming. We're crockery
slipped to the edge of a tilting table but so slowly
    who'd notice, until...?
That clatter's not the bells of Dunwich
three miles out, not the family silver being rifled,
more like cutlery shrugged into stainless-steel vats
    behind canteen roller-blinds
in a hospital no one can see their way out of,
or the school you're always back at in your dreams,
or the idea of the Self, or the United Kingdom plc,
    you know, any crumbling institution.

A Scorcher

Walk, don't jog: it's official.
Don't let the kids play out.
Don't breathe the air. Reactions
simmered in a pan of ozone smog

dissolve our boundaries; across the *life/
not-life* line molecules begin to fraternise
like a breaking of ranks in the trenches.
So we cough and slow.

We cover up. Overexposed
we check for shadows on the skin.
In the ultraviolet light of what we know
the future begins to look pale

as the Middle Ages. Grey-faced girls
with thighs no wider than their knees
appear in our midst now
like omens of famine, bruise-eyed

like the worn-down wives
they'd rather die than be.
And we learn to adapt. Betray
no more than awkward sympathy

when someone's toddler in the crowded bus
fights a strangle of asthma,
scrabbling and slipping on each breath
like a loosening scree.

Persons Unknown

This is the Pier Point Hotel and they

are the only residents.
It's more exclusive now than 5-star

since the Council whacked up hardboard
on the downstairs, and the UNSAFE STRUCTURE sign.

The Receiver's got his hands full, what
with weighing an antheap of debts

against goods that get less with each slither
of shale, each crump of a wave on the cliff.

It was a wet night they teased back the wire
just enough for a calor gas stove and a bedroll

and themselves. By morning the flit of them
at an upstairs window and that cat-at-the-back-door

baby's cry was proof, if proof were needed:
once land starts slipping it goes to the bad,

good riddance. Remember how the Clifftop Bar
broke out in an acne of under-age drinking

and the landlord took to serving in his vest,
his cheeks rusting from the inside like a wreck

at high-water? Now these fly-by-night squatters
had a cranked-out bus, one with sacks on the windows

and a dog like frayed wire, didn't they? Well, no,
but these things soon appeared

somewhere nearby where no one could see them.

*

It may be the Pier Point Hotel but you

don't figure, you're a blank
on the inventory. You
among fixtures and fittings

like the cherry plush bar
with its paunched look, its buttons
gone missing like teddy bears' eyes.

Yes, you, putting your boots up
in the cork tiled alcoves,
you, squelching the pump handles

(marked with a price per pint
that nails their last pull to the month
sure as carbon dating.)

Kicking the steel kegs, you,
you'd sup the dregs, you'd spoon them
to the baby when it creaks by night.

Why don't you answer? Or appear
at a balcony window like royalty, to bless us
with a V-sign? Thanks to you

folk lie awake all hours, listening
for the raves you must surely
foment out of nowhere

like maggots in meat. Why can't we hear?

*

Final guests of the Pier Point Hotel we

go on tiptoe for no reason.
Or spread arms and whoosh
down the corridor laughing
as if there were maids stepping out

from every bedroom, tea things
shocked up off their trays
like a clatter of doves.
But the kid can't be left

in a room stacked with bust chairs
and pieces of bidet, where moonlight
still winkles out glass from the floorboards
or flatters the gold-look

of a wire record rack
full of *Swing with the Sixties
Volume 3*. We can't talk
but must whisper or shout,

and the closer we bundle to sleep,
the more apart we seem.
Last night each of us thought we woke
to find the other missing

and knew where to look: through the door
we shouldn't open to the Clifftop Bar,
with no window, no frame and no wall
where the mould-patterned Axminster frays

in a bite like stringy celery.
At our feet, a faint whicker of gulls...
A few slipped off to circle leisurely
as cream in stirred coffee. Beneath

rose a pale blotch of foam.
When I was small in bed
I'd squeeze my eyelids tight,
half afraid of the space in my head

where the nebulas came like that and kept on coming.

Postcards, West Bay

(after a photograph by Martin Parr)

These are the last days. And these are the signs.
    And nothing is by chance.
These are the cards, the Tarot of the times.
    We shuffle, heads bent,
round the white wire racks. These wayside shrines.

These icons. Faithfulness on its settee
    is figured by The Poodle
gazing where the coal-look fire must be,
    his master's voice. The same
fire lights The Fluffy Kitten's eyes, though she

is a type of the Snow Leopard, captured
    at the entrails of her prey,
a party streamer tangle. Here is The Thatcher
    on the crest of his new fire risk,
hand raised like the poodle's paw. What rapture

is prepared for him, for all who understand
    the correspondences: the buffed-
up green steam locomotive and the two-in-hand
    plough team converging
on a final point? The point is where we stand

in late light, colours heightened, sights for sore
    eyes, eczema'd.
Salve us. Everything we see is slightly raw.
    Don't scratch the surface,
it'll scar. Who made the red shift, and what for,

what hopes and brochures drew us to West Bay
    (Look to the West. The West
declines.) and booked us in and made us stay
    and made us see how everything
bleeds, bleed, these last days, bleeds away.

A Liminal State

(Estonia, September 1994)

1 *Documentary*

Five Aeroflot sky-tubs by the lumpy runway
sport blue-and-white paint now: ESTONIAN AIR.
Like gulls with a storm in the offing
they face the same way at the wind.

There are trains cut in half at the border
like worms; an independent engine
pulls out from the platform while its rolling stock
stays Russian. Lines have to be drawn

like today: PAKA *(bye for now,*
not quite *adieu)* flyposts most walls
with a Red Army helipad cap, a walrus neck
that seems an easy target from behind.

Like kids with their parents' cameras
there are families posed edgily outside
the place people tried not to mention,
with a name plate saying anything but KGB.

The barracks is a film set waiting
for a new producer and a cast of thousands.
The windows are kicked out from the inside,
bunk rooms trashed. Here's half a skip of uniforms.

Round the base, there's been a fly-buzz of types
in leather jackets all this last year,
men in a small way of business but expanding
and with foreign friends. Out there in the bay

ochre hulks have faced home up the Gulf of Finland
for months as if waiting the word.
(The Moscow-Tallinn post goes quicker
these days via London.)

Beneath the stained ziggurat
of the Olympic Pride yachting complex
a sharp Finnish hydrofoil suns its wings.
A car ferry trots out in the team's new colours

and is not yet anybody's news.

2 *The Bronze Age*

A nod, in passing, to the scar
in the park where all the paths
     converge on nothing
but a ten-foot concrete square
gouged up like a bad extraction,
shreds of tooth, steel nerve-ends
     sheared off proud
to the ground, not safe for children.
It nags like the place where the pain
has been and gone, the lost limb
     still tapping its fingers,
still humming the old refrain.

There's a clutch of Lenins in the cellar
of the town museum, faced everywhichway
     to the future, some reclining,
most declaiming, deafly. Quite a conspiracy...
Still, their splintered soles would slot
back onto the scars of their plinths
     snug as a numb foot
in a snowboot. They're kept, no, not
just in case, for as long as it takes
for History to lose that old capital H
     like a crime on its head,
for all this to be lower-case, just history.

One night the Bronze Age began. A van
skulked up an alley finger-picking clean
        every public memorial.
Slogans stuttered into silence. Scrap men
made a killing. The great names and dates
lost their memory, letter by letter,
        leaving pinholes in the slabs
like Braille, or the undeciphered script
in the newly-excavated sanctum, which might
if you let your focus blur, just fall
        into pattern and sense.
Might be a curse, the writing on the wall.

3 *Liminal*

The rackety bus has shaken us down
like a washing machine soothes fretful

babies, down to there-there mutterings
on the edge of sleep, so low I can't tell

which is Estonian, which Russian. Straight
cut through flat land, the road's as dull

as the proof that Zeno's arrow never strikes.
There's a tree without a trunk, a stonepile

like a reef, in low mist. Puddles
of brightness rise as darkness falls,

in measure like a physical equation.
Memories of marsh seep back, subliminal,

till it's white to the black rim of woods
under darkening blue, like the national

flag. In one already-changing moment
droplet after droplet casts its individual

vote to be mist. The road is a causeway
waiting for a wave of it to curl

up and over. Now. We hit the brightness
and we're in it and it's gloom and chill

and half the night to go. The driver hums
to keep awake, no words, all

low throat voice, no tune.

4 *International Relations*

The deep-pile hush
of moss. All round us
tingling resonance of spruce.
I can't utter a word
for fear it lasts and lasts.

'You English,' she says,
'I can't tell from American
these days, always rushing in
to share your feelings.
This heart on the sleeve

(is that right?) can't still
be beating... Friendship?
The official word for occupation.
Give me fifty years
to lose the taste of it,

I'm sorry...' And later:
'No wonder your Americans
and Russians understand each other
like the best of enemies.
They're so alike,

the type who invite you,
surprise! to a party
in your own house.
If you say you have a headache
they look hurt – *sincerely* –

then kick down the door...'

5 *Scorched Earth*

A year or two
of thistles uncut
and it's theirs:

first, nettles
at the borders, bramble
tripwires, then birches

like fingers of dazzle
prising in between
the warping timbers

to a hayloft's
warm biscuity dark.
Too white, those trees

stepping in over marginal land
between the forest
and the straight-ruled wheat –

too bright, as if
they sucked light up
to flare it off

like a Statue-of-Liberty
torch at the oil works,
smoke by day and fire by night,

and the earth at their feet
too dark-grained
fifty years on – the ash

of hayloft, house and barn
feeding grass, feeding
birch and bramble, feeding

thistles as sharp as a cough
in a theatre's hush
before the next act starts.

6 Forest Brother

(*Metsavennad:* Forest Brothers – resistance fighters
against the Soviet occupation of 1944)

Consider the last of the Forest Brothers

thirty years behind bars
of spruce or white birch trunks
that look like a cage from any angle.
Thirty years of melting through.

Of nesting in the needly itch
like the last of a species
listed as extinct
but still with a price on his pelt.

Of the plush smell of mushrooms
on the edge of rotting
and the rush-matting drift
underfoot and the moss,

such a hush, just a cough
and the wood catches cold.
Consider living like a mouse
in the soundbox of a violin

among the wind's harmonics,
being what isn't there
at the edge of the clearing
when the dogs bark and the farmer

chooses not to hear. His war
comes down to this: to be a dream,
a bad one, moving in the corner
of the vision of a dawn

that has abolished shadows.
Do dreams itch? Catch cold?
Or look up by a river,
with a rucksack and a leather jacket

grinning at two fishermen
who pass the time of day
and then produce a camera, smile!
and then their KGB credentials.

August Sabe. 1979.
His last word is a gulp of air
in the pool where he jumped
and stayed under. Consider him

then consider the last
Forest Brother but one, who died
some time earlier, thinking
'There's still Sabe' – him

with no name, no photograph,
so much more rare
because he could be anyone…

7 *In the Bar of the Writers' Union*

Back in the bad old days
    I had a job – to say everything
        no one else would. And they listened
like kids in a Whispering Gallery
    half afraid of their own voices
        scuttling round blank walls and back.
I said too much, of course.
    Even a little was too much –
        these were the bad old days, remember –
and when the silencers came
    my hush rippled through crowds;
        when I passed down the street
folk turned to listen.
    Ah, the bad old days. Now
        I can leave a silence and...

That was one, did you notice it?
    No?
        Then I'll say it again.

8 *Postsoviet Postmodern*
Vaike-Oismae, Tallinn

Launched by the Soviet Sixties, this scheme
for a suburb in concentric rings says moon-base,
says orbiting station: a hand-me-down dream
    from American sci-fi. Remember the Space Race?
    Cosmonauts on launchpads in the Khazakh
    dust, pot-roasted secretly at the state's
discretion? Now we wake to stains and cracks,
the creep of concrete cancer much the same
as relicts of the Sixties anywhere: Caracas,
    Wandsworth. But vineberry swarms up to claim
    ten storey cliffs, each creeper a ripped seam
    of autumn. Each block wears a shirt of flame.

The Pumping Station's down again; half
Tallinn's hot taps gurgle dry. I'm in an eighth
floor flat, bussed to a cousin's for a bath.
          On TV, a Mexican dream of L.A.: ghost-
          Spanish moves the lips. Curt as an epitaph,
          Estonian subtitles. Russian, dubbed almost
in synch. Slipped through cracks in the scene
a stray *porque?* like a weed in a pavement. My host
has left *Women's Day: Australia's Biggest Magazine*
          (from other cousins) where I'll see. *'Aussie Man Relates
          Penis Mutilation' 'Diana – Sexpot Or Ice Queen?'*
          with a Japanese remote control for paperweight.

Outside, there's scrub encroaching. Waste ground.
A cow at a stake. A dirt track. And a frontier
with what's gone. That low grassed-over mound
          should be a long barrow, but the door
          is dented steel – a reinforced surround,
          a man-sized catflap. Now we're echoes in a corridor,
an air-raid-shelter hush one step could detonate,
but lined with lock-ups, dozens, like a bullion store.
Ours rattles up, bumping its counterweight,
          a cylinder block, and there's the family car,
          the great grey Lada like a warrior in state
          among shelves racked with gravegoods, jar on jar
of gherkin flesh crammed into murky green.
Lab specimens. And garnet glints: a ruined bar
of bottles – vodka, 'Churchill's London Gin' –
          transfused with redcurrant juice, like every year
          in every farm's earth-cellar till the history machine
          crashed from the sky and left us stranded here.

Babble

He never asked –
how could he? –
but it came with him,
the gift of tongues,

and they clustered around
as if astounded,
total strangers bending
to his buggy in the street.

Those with ears to hear
might spot Inuit gutturals,
sheaves of Slavonic *tsh* or *tsch*,
a glottal click of Xhosa

tangled like all our routes
out of Africa, forkings of tongues
into deltas and floodplains.
They became afraid

and held up things,
simple and solid to cling to.
Teddy, they said, *baby*,
mouthing slow and clear

like trained negotiators
hotlined to the penthouse
where he'd holed up, Howard Hughes
of the Babel Hotel

amongst hung gardens
and the hammering of gastarbeiter
workmen; some nights
a whole storey gives way;

in the morning there's scaffolding,
power tools, Michael Jackson songs
in Turkish, all channels at once
on their trannies. No wonder

that there comes a day
he chucks it in, throwing the switch
to cut whole sectors into darkness,
silence, and comes down

to their smiles and their camcorders
whirring like the press corps
when his lips or tongue chance
on a Ma or Da.

Cut, Cut

The programme's in the can. That's me, cut clean.
Forget the out-takes tangling in the bin
like the mating of worms. Forget them, the dumb-
struck, the stumbling, a night-shelter full, like the hum
after the Late News, Shipping Forecast, Close Down...
                    Quick, tune
me to another channel, easy listening, where a non-
stop DJ is driving his studio through till dawn
till his lights clip a hitchhiker miles from nowhere
mouthing things at the dark, but he won't pull over,
would you? Would you wind the window down:
                    hey, kid, jump in?

The Language of the Bird People

unmoved
out on the edge of utter
North
    of utter
        utter...
            (try again)

unmoved
thin as lace-

makers' bobbins
their limb-silhouettes

against a grey lake
in their punts of bark so flat

they might be standing on the water
they compose an alphabet

with the tilt of a spear
the coil of a cast net

splash
though all that reaches here

at the edge is ripples
broad and shallow

truckling at a boulder
a stipple of reeds

like a visible rumour
then again

the peewit cries they scratch
on the frosted glass of morning

once an hour maybe
unmoving is a message

cut in lapidary style
that spells precisely nothing

we can hope   but try
again   to guess

'Cult objects: Neolithic proto-
Finno-Ugric'
                a bird-headed ladle
                the rim of a bowl
incised with Diver Pintail Grebe
each reduced
                to an ideogram
                a glyph   a rune
ten species of Z evolving to
                pure attitude

'A religion of waterfowl, presumably'
the reappearing
                W or V of geese
                like a sign in the sky
ragged edge of the season's much-
patched garment
                that they stitch
                back into place
with needling cries   to make do
                for another year

Don't credit the tale
that they followed the wild-
fowl north so far
they left speech behind

like a Victorian explorer's
folding table, candlesticks and cloth
abandoned almost sadly
by the last defecting porter.

But whistles and caws
are sharper warnings, honks and chirrups
more companionable
for meaning only that.

Don't think their poets
whittled nightingale cadenzas.
No, picture them rapt
in a darkening ring

by the sound of one goose
cronking with a micro-tonal
change of pitch
less than a warping of windspeed

till in a trance beyond boredom
they were seized
by the wonder of distance, thoughts
teased into cirrus-thin threads.

On a poor night they might plan
new destinations; on a good one,
woken by a rush of wings,
might find the poet gone.

strakings of cirrus

the windpaths
down which birds will come

today?   no

till the folk brim full of it
this lacking something

and the wide high sky

is one turbulent stream
of not arriving

the cloud teased to slaloming tracks

prickling smitters of sand
swerving over a beach

a live white shadow

they squint north
as if they could see

in the switch and tease

of wind direction
something   something

call it home

'Tenth night out: serious tundra, bog-
quaking soft. Lashed guyropes to stones.
No chat. By this stage of an expedition
talking's as much of a slog
      as walking, and less use. Dusk was a seep
      of grey light downwards, puddling in a tarn
      edged with boulders, crosshatched with reeds.
      The other men clocked into sleep

and missed it: up over the moor
from the south, a creaking
like a waggon being trundled, then
as sudden as the kicking open of a door
      the tarn was a clamour, a claque
      in the front stalls of darkness,
      each separate syllable insisting
      on itself, a shopfloor clang and crack

of hammering out the likeness
of a language. A raw spring of speech.
I stumbled out, my torch beam stubbing
into bristling wings like the pikes
      of a pitchfork rebellion as their outcry spread
      across the water, circles shuddering
      out and all the voices leaving and the Word,
      if word it was, unsaid…'

    ⊐══◗

At some point on the road north,
a divorce
and another and another…
Steps to more crisp articulation.

One group holds north-west
is the true way of the birdpaths,
one hears the wind in the east.
A turn of speech

might sway a council
like a change in the breeze,
one leading to a sibilance of spruces,
one to the vowel of a duck cry,

while the dumb Ob
widens its swerves into marshland
without end or definition.
The Nenets. The Komi. The Khanty.

Each arrives at a name, one word
finally uttered. At the logging camp
an old man washing pans
feeds a girl from the Institute's

microphone with syllables
from his grandmother's larder.
He steals the cassete player
for his nephews in Murmansk

and the end of the line
is a footnote. The Udmuts.
The Mordvin. The Mansi.
Did they know they'd arrived

and there was nothing for it but to wait,
unmoving, for the chainsaws
ruling a new edge to the forest,
new smoke rising, uttered

once, and losing definition
as it thins towards them
like geese of a dwindling species
trying for true North

                    again
                         again?

That Grave, Heptonstall Churchyard

(for Tracy)

I'm not here now; you've never been
        and she?
She's here in name. Put in her place.
All round her, life on life's defined
        by family:

Beloved Husband... Wife Of The Above...
        And dates,
the years from *Sadly Missed* to *Reunited.*
Here it's life that puts asunder; death
        consolidates

but still needs edging. There's a splashy blurt
        of strimmer. Smells
of cut green. Her plot's earth, no kerb,
a give-and-take of weeds along the border.
        Now the bells

blur, two notes slipping out of phase
        that jar
like two tongues round one language, half
a tone apart, like English and American
        in you, in her –

half rhymes, the way your lips make *marry*
        sound like *merry.*
So the continental drift of vowels
and lives breeds ironies, which epitaphs
        are meant to bury.

I'm not here, not now, but writing this
        upstairs, alone
and with you, also not here, in the way
that words can do, the kind that won't be
        set in stone.

Around the church graves lie like hatches
      battened down.
In place. Does she belong? Do we? Where
else could these thoughts be at home but on
      disputed ground?

Fern Charm

Protect us from the rage of ferns,
from the baby's clenched fist,
from the cobra's hood. From the spring

of the set trap, from the slippy
grip-curl of octopus limbs,
protect us. Say *Hart's-tongue*

Hart's-tongue as if words
might lick the newborn
season into shape. Protect us

from the Spring.

Mock Orange

Keep it, he thought, and watch it wither.
A controlled experiment.

A tissue sample, tested
to destruction. Science against sentiment.

It was limp in a week; in a month,
crisp as a wing case in the spider's nook;

in two, a Haversham gown
already, with that age-scorched look,

no scent, so little body
to its parchment, the touch of a pen

would destroy it. There, it's gone.
But it's not. He starts over again.

*

Evaluate. Record. Two, three hours of seminar.
A working lunch. A breath outside,
and a throwaway line, a dare, and there they are

with a sprig each from someone else's garden;
back for two, three hours more
of what he can't remember, can't remember anything

except how she twirled hers, absently,
stroking the curve of her throat while listening,
down to the dip between the collar bones. He

found his still in his hand, and hid it, coming home.

*

Keep it, he thought, and watch it wither.
Now it's scentless, colourless,
QED, stick to science; resist
temptation to play alchemist,

to pound it in a mortar, to a white
dust potent as cocaine,
the flower of albescence, something
dying for a change.

No, let it wither, husks of flight
like the butterfly wings
good children used to save to press
into pictures of quite other things,

ball gowns, waterfalls – that
was the art of it. Under glass
they're antiques now, and the children
more gone than the butterflies. Let it pass...

                        *

...or with its own dried twig
like a pin through the thorax,
classify it. But tonight it's him
the collector who's nailed to the page,
squirming, just out of reach

of his numbing formaldehyde,
while the wings of all the moments
caught, or not quite, whisper
in the air around him, taunting.
One brushes his cheek.

Hungry Ghosts in Happy Eater

These two, wanting so much
they could eat each other
up, all up
and they'd be gone

leaving what
for the damage assessors,
the investigators,
but a napkin

crumpled like the story of a life
neatly dropped on a plate
and food uneaten
and the bill unpaid

and two chairs facing,
empty to the brim
with wants
like the guests

at a spoilt kid's party
wide-eyed
as the rabbit-mould
pink jelly, cut,

slumps like a last
chance missed
to tense and twitch
and leap away?

One stage on the Tibetan Wheel of Life is occupied by the Hungry Ghosts;
with huge stomachs and tiny mouths, they can never satisfy their hungers.

Time Lapse

Already going, it may have been gone
  before he'd raised a glass –
    absent friends:

the midnight that wouldn't be hers
  for eight hours yet was off
    sweeping west,

sweeping brilliant moments, congas, party
  popper tangle, fireworks falling,
    Auld Lang Syne

into its bin bag; off-road, over hills now, over
  cloggy levels and the shot-silk silt fields
    of the estuary,

a radio mast, a lightship rocked by the Atlantic.
  Sweeping foam tips up like sawdust,
    broken glass

and resolutions, now it panned its beam
  of dark across, a time-zone wide,
    not remembering

him to her or anyone to anyone, as if
  forgetting was its job. A year
    between us now,

he thought, and what if time, once slipped,
  went on slipping? If he slept
    he might open his eyes

to find it decades or a different life,
  a bed round which, uneasy,
    unfamiliar

wife and children watch him wake, afraid
  as for a moment he can't
    recollect himself.

Hard Water

Hard water
has been through the hill.
The taste is learned, not something it was born with.

A traveller thrown down a well –
you know how it goes: there's a lamp
and by its light we know

this it must be a story, with an ending.
The tale of hard water
is not one of those.

You can hold on for only so long
and say that this is waiting,
then let go

not knowing if bedrock will open
and draw you on through, not
knowing how long,

and how hard, and whether
what you would be then
would still be you.

*

A bare ridge with its bones showing,
empty-pocket valleys... *Karst.*
He tastes the *k* of it, correct and fine
as the dry-white edge to the water,
vintage straight from the tap
in a toothmug on the bedside table.
She lulls herself to sleep
with *swallet.*

One moment it's there, then it's not:
the word slips underground.
There's a scuffling edge; if you catch
the warning of that hollow sound
you're already too close. Miles away,
a fold of dale leaks lush
green out of nowhere, sundew,
and you can't see why.

*

Hard water
won't lather. Hotel soap
skids off it, won't mix,
swirls in the en suite basin
in a mist or lies, sweet scum,

along the surface in a jasmine-
scented slick.
He stirs it with his fingers,
frisks and frisks;
the froth won't come.

*

Say a negative sculptor shaped
those hollowed spaces in the heart of stone:
a tusk of dark here, here a wavy *kris*,
a narwhal horn, a flute, a fluke, a bone.

Say a negative writer made a book
of wormholes that when shut composed
a sphere like the dance of electrons;
when opened, nothing was exposed.

Say that two lovers lived in a story
too far from the common light of day.
Say that what can't be seen, can't be.
Say that... no, just don't say.

*

A Melamine kettle on a short leash.
As he runs the tap he catches sight
of sickly fur, a hardening of arteries.
    It's becoming a cave,

secreting limestone, stalactite material
like the caddis-fly-larva-ghost tubes
growing down under bridges, that might be
    pale roots from above

but shatter faintly, wetly, at a touch,
just tubes of water, with a scale skin,
a naked bud quivering: something
    has got to give.

*

There are stories that surface passim in this landscape,
any pub, any guest house breakfast: the dog

down a pothole, a yelp and it's gone;
a week, it's washed out of a cave five miles away

half skinned, starved and shuddering. *Yes, but ...*
he finds himself thinking. ...*when the owner*

came to claim it? Could it ever be

quite his again? And why, this morning,
does he find himself telling her the other, the one

with the diver, though she doesn't want to hear?
It's true, he keeps saying, as if that's a reason.

Imagine. Walkie-talkie crackle back at base;
for a moment they cheer: he's breached a furthest

chamber, dizzily vaulted, a *cathedrale engloutie*,

then a pause. The air gauge.
One third there, one back and one

for safety: that's the Rule of Three

he's broken, and he knows. Imagine. Then:
I won't die struggling in the sump. Imagine

him, space walker, pushing off almost weightless,
rising through vaults and columns. And them.

The time it takes. From nowhere they've seen
or will see (the cave will be sealed), his voice

fainter but calm, saying: *don't go; talk to me.*

           *

Interpenetration each of each,
lime-stiffened water, porous stone:

last night I caught a look of yours
on my own face and felt myself dissolving

knowing I'd leach through you, you
through me and each come out alone.

Tact

(Dr Sun-Yat-Sen Garden, Vancouver)

A floating leaf pokes up its head,
a lacquered eye stripe, and becomes a terrapin.
     Each pebble is deliberate:
sharp/white for yang, smooth/black for yin.

Outside the tile-topped walls a crane,
wires, intersection lights... Inside, waist high
     raddled limestone
in a tank of stillness – bonsai

mountains. Though if those
are mountains how huge are the carp that rise
     through the pools? And me?
A giant suddenly embarrassed by his size.

Can't budge... till in the courtyard,
slow as dancing underwater, Tai Chi Chuan
     unwraps the movements of its doers
like an endless present. One young man,

sea-urchin-haired, with droopy dungarees
unhitched on one side, stoops and sweeps and smooths
     the space around him. Out,
along his gaze, the movement moves

beyond his finger-tips, a cast
coil, as if silt-thick eddies veered and stirred
     the liquid time has slowed to.
Tact: to be, precisely, when a word

might break the surface tension
like a not-yet-lover's not-quite-accidental touch,
     the shudder that runs through a life
and moves on, out. I've said too much.

Ground Control

A gust, and the skyline is bristling with them,
cloud-slip behind them and wild blue bluster,
and what are they hefting, one-handed like butlers

with trays of champagne flutes? Blades
of six-foot wingspans like well-balanced spears,
light as bird bone, and damsel fly bodies, cerise,

white, kingfisher, lime. Up close, it is a tribe
of married-looking men in specs and mufflers,
like a Scout troop from the Fifties. With the bluff

drop at their feet, the motorway miles down,
and the wind, they take a roll call, surnames only
then step to the edge. At the whistle they go,

leaning forwards, balancing each model glider
on the air, nose up, nose down, to teeter,
then edge out of reach. Out of whisper.

A single line sketch of itself, one turns
as easily as frisking over in your sleep to run
downwind, shaving the ridge, and the men

come tracking downhill at a slant, in pairs,
across heather and ash and burnt gorse curls
and violets. With black box and whiskery aerial,

eyes on the sky, each one trusts the other's
two hands on his waist to steer him, leaning
heads together, whispering like secrets

where to, and where now to, put his feet.

Summerhouse Sauna

Men, we don't touch.
Even a handshake is a brisk clunk
like a gear change –
the crisper, the less ground lost.

Here there's nothing between us.
See our buttock-marks in sweat
flank to flank on the wooden slat shelf.
We're racked like loaves in an oven;

this could be some lesser waiting-room
in Hell, lit by the glimmer
of the bow-legged stove
that squats like a grudge in armour.

A dip of the copper ladle
in the bucket, a splash on the pigs
of scrap iron that stand in for stones,
and steam takes us all by the throat.

For a moment we're boggle-eyed
all in the same no-language.
The first word anyone has breath for
is a victory and goes down like a joke.

Outside, we lope down to a pool
edged in bin-liner black
as if we'd evaded the hunt. Unmanned,
scrotum shrunk to a prune,

we gasp, duck and come up to mist
in the birches, that sparkles the skin
of the pond, and our own pink as babies.
We could start again from here.

Underside

Lit from below

the pale grey-green of lichen,
our faces drift away

and away from ourselves
much as our rowboat drifts

beneath this shallow arch
that has stalactite dewlaps already.

In a hush like a studio
suddenly on air, a drip

sends its ripples out
up from under our faces

and this low vault and the blades
of our shipped and still dribbling oars,

the way we play stray lights
across each other – threat or love

like the flash of a car in the street
riffled back through a chink in the curtains...

Yes, but quite indifferently.
I can't help looking for the spot

where long after the drop
the rings keep coming

into being, light
out of dark out of light,

although you'd think there's nothing there.

Gargangel

It began as a creaking, an ache in my stone
thews. There's a word for you,
since words are all I've got from over-
looking centuries: gossip, hey-nonny-no
and paternoster. Acid rain and organ wheeze
had worn me down to bone and horn and wing,

to a crick in the neck and a joke of a wing
like a broken umbrella. Still, to be set in stone
seemed like a future. Whose clever wheeze
was it to set me trembling? And did you
so much as frisk your hair or look up, downcast? No,
it could have been a small cloud passing over,

my shadow touching you. Then it was over
until, after dark, the first twinge in my wing,
a thin sinew unlocking. No, I said, no,
I've seen it: crash; next morning, shattered stone
and the precinct taped off. Not me, thank you.
Figures my age are meant to spout and wheeze

but not like this, not this bump-start wheeze
inside my ribs. I thought all that was over
centuries ago, that ridiculous *It could be you...*
from empty skies: How long since an angel wing-
beat last rattled the stained glass? Stone
the crows, what are you made of? Could I say *No*,

leave me to crouch and crumble slowly? No!
I struggled upright, with a rip and wheeze,
uprooted, with a shower of dust and stone
and for a moment I swayed, teetering over
the stomach-punch drop, then unfurled a wing
and launched out, where else but towards you,

amazed, aloft, alone, as much I as you are you.
Dipping badly over Pulteney Street, no
turning back now, I cranked up a wing
beat, stiff, slow, with a whistle like the wheeze
of pigeon panic. No one looked up as I passed over
homing on your sill, your narrow window, stone

clunking stone and clinging, peering in – and saw you
squinting up, over your reading glasses. Now! But no,
I squ-squ-wheeze but can't fit in, can't fold this wing.

Hanging Garden

If I did it again, it would have to be there

in Devonian Gardens, in the warp and weft
    of downtown Calgary.

The street map's not much use. That square
    of green; it's nowhere, literally,

on earth. Get there, the sign points skywards.
    You'd come, wouldn't you,

in white, beside me, in the stainless lift,
    slipping up its glass tube

snug as the plunger in a hypodermic?
    Three, four storeys high

among mirrorshade windows pixelating
    one another and the sky,

a seasick sway as gravity relaxes, then
    we'd step out, you and I,

into rainforest. Insect fibrillations. Fountains
    like whippy ice cream.

In the recycled plosh, dazed koi. The garden,
    hanging, cradled by technology,

held for its own protection in a girder cage
    with all workings exposed,

no pretence: thrumming ducts thick as dustbins,
    fan-blowers in rows

sigh like jet engines trundling to takeoff,
    fan blades idling, as if this

were aircraft, hangar *and* departure lounge.
  Any moment now, the shift

of pitch, the surge, the caught breath. Squeeze
  my hand, whoever you might be,

and lead me past the crimson rope, the Private
  Function sign, where hourly

the brides and the grooms take their places
  and glow, and something

like the first time ever is preserved; photographers
  make summer lightning

and glimpsed through undergrowth are faces, some
  just passing, some returning

day after day among the spikes and fronds
  and bougainvillea to yearn in,

it could be at us. My unknowable future,
  what couldn't we swear

in all innocence? Yes, we'd say, yes.
  It would have to be there.

TONBRIDGE SCHOOL SMYTHE LIBRARY